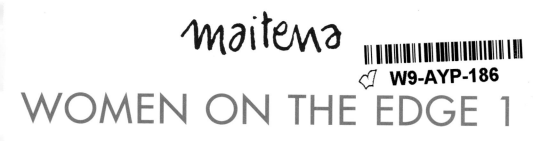

# maitena

# WOMEN ON THE EDGE 1

**RIVERHEAD BOOKS**
**NEW YORK**

RIVERHEAD BOOKS
Published by The Berkley Publishing Group
A division of Penguin Group (USA) Inc.
375 Hudson Street
New York, New York 10014

WOMEN ON THE EDGE 1

Previously published in Spanish by Lumen, S.A.: March 2003
First Riverhead trade paperback edition: September 2004
Riverhead trade paperback ISBN: 1-59448-080-X

This book has been catalogued with the Library of Congress.

Printed in the United States of America

10 9 8 7 6 5 4 3 2 1

To my children, Amaya and Juan, my first readers.
To Daniel Divinsky, my first editor.
And to Carlitos, my only patron.

# EDGINESS
## PECULIAR
### TO HER SEX

# Six typically feminine things

# Some of the most common prejudices concerning women

# Six things that upset a woman

# The only six things women envy about men

# Things you notice when it starts getting hot

# While on vacation, get some rest

# What do women expect when they get to the beach?

# Frequent paranoias

# Six common aches and pains

# Eight things women do when they're depressed

SHOP FOR CLOTHES...

I'LL take it

...THEY WOULDN'T BE CAUGHT DEAD IN.

GET THEIR HAIR STYLED...

GB

...BEYOND REPAIR.

LOOK IN THE MIRROR...

...AND GOUGE THEIR SKIN.

SLEEP LIKE A LOG, EAT LIKE A PIG...

CRUNCH! CRUNCH!

...THEN WALLOW IN GUILT.

WRITE LONG LETTERS...

Sniff! Sniff!

...That they'll never send.

CALL THEIR FRIENDS...

HELLO! HELLO?

...AND HANG UP WHEN THEY ANSWER.

LISTEN TO VERY SAD MUSIC...

...TO MAKE THEMSELVES FEEL WORSE.

ASK THEMSELVES IMPOSSIBLE QUESTIONS...

so then what?

...JUST TO ANSWER NO!

# Six out of a thousand difficult things to explain . . .

# Six difficult moments in a woman's life

# The most frequent "famous last words"

# A woman's life is full of doubts...

# Things women have had to master to prove they aren't stupid, as time goes by . . .

# PHYSICAL
## ALTERATIONS
### AND OTHER FASHION TRENDS

# Women are so beautiful . . . !

# Six great beauty injustices

# Nobody talks about menstruation . . .
## but it's on everyone's mind!

# Six dreadful moments in a woman's life

# The fashion this season is great!

# Illogical and ecological fashion trends are in!

# Several good reasons to start a diet

# Life is not fair

# Carnival parade? No! Fall fashion exclusives!

# How to be fashionable
# with whatever is in your closet

# Common aesthetic disputes
# between men and women

# A TIMELESS DILEMMA:
## COUPLES

# Six reasons why women marry men

# The six worst defects in a man

# Six ways to treat a husband

# Six things men generally hate

# Some things he'll never know about

# Those things only women can say
## (because if men say them, they've had it!)

# Six ways to put down your partner

# The six people who threaten him

# Little things that make men impossible to live with

# Love is dead when...

# Six things to do after a breakup

# Six good reasons to see your ex

# Some reasons why fewer people are getting married

# Four good reasons never to get married

# How long does love last? As time goes by . . .

# CONSTANT CHANGE:
## THE FAMILY

# Six fears of pregnant women

# Six behavioral patterns
# typical of moms with small babies

# The things kids request as they grow up

# Common blunders made by people who don't have kids

# Back to school . . .

# Tell me what you've lost,
# and I'll tell you who you are.

# A few precious moments between father and daughter

# Six unforgettable moments on vacation

# Six foolproof signs
# your teenage daughter is normal

# Six foolproof signs your teenage son is normal

# How late a daughter can stay out, as time goes by . . .

# A boy, his mom and the spanking, as time goes by . . .

# Six types of mother-in-law

AND A FEW OTHER THINGS THAT
# DRIVE US CLOSER
## TO THE EDGE

# The thrill of not knowing
## exactly where you're going

# Six foolproof ways to stay warm at night

# Six good reasons to lose sleep

# Six risks frequently associated with birthday parties

# Redecorating can be fun!

# Things that inevitably conk out at the same time

# Enemies of your vacation

# Christmas shopping is fun!

# Typical remarks made on New Year's eve

# Topics of conversation
# when there's nothing to talk about

# Family evaluation of the prospective son-in-law, as time goes by . . .

# "What do you want to be when you grow up?" as time goes by . . .

# The happy cook's six worst enemies

# What men and women first notice when they go into a restaurant

I WAS BORN IN 1962, I THINK. BECAUSE I WAS THE SIXTH OF SEVEN SIBLINGS AND MY MOM HAD LITTLE TIME TO REMEMBER INSIGNIFICANT DETAILS.

COME ON, MARI... LOLI... ANI... CARLI... RAM... PA...

MAITENA

FROM EARLY CHILDHOOD, I TRIED TO LEAD A NORMAL LIFE.

...BUT I WAS NO GOOD AT SPORTS, I FOUND SCHOOL BORING

AND I WAS TOO MUCH OF A FEMINIST TO BECOME A HOUSEMAKER

SO, I BEGAN DRAWING TO KEEP MYSELF BUSY. AT MY HOUSE, IF YOU DIDN'T KEEP BUSY, THERE WAS ALWAYS A CHORE WAITING FOR YOU.

...SO, THAT'S HOW I DISCOVERED, THAT WHILE I WAS DRAWING, MY THOUGHTS COULD ROAM FREE, WITHOUT ANYONE ATTEMPTING TO EDUCATE ME.

SO MUCH THINKING MADE ME REALIZE THAT, IF EVER I MARRIED, I WOULD NEVER BE AN INDEPENDENT WOMAN.

STILL I GOT MARRIED, BECAUSE HE UNDERSTOOD MY JOKES.

(UNFORTUNATELY THAT WAS ALL HE UNDERSTOOD)

I WAS ONLY 17 AND WAS ALREADY BEING PUBLISHED IN THOSE WAITING-ROOM MAGAZINES!

BY 19, I ALREADY HAD TWO WONDERFUL KIDS, THREE LOUSY JOBS, ALL SORT OF PROBLEMS...

AND GRAY HAIR!

I SEPARATED AT 24

I WAS TOO YOUNG FOR THAT MUCH RESPONSIBILITY

I DECIDED MY LIFE LACKED SOME SEX, DRUGS AND ROCK'N'ROLL

I DON'T REMEMBER MUCH ABOUT THE NEXT FEW YEARS

BUT I USED RED HENNA IN MY HAIR

MY DRAWINGS BEGAN TO SHOW UP IN RACY MAGAZINES IN THE FORM OF EROTIC COMICS. I ALSO ILLUSTRATED CHILDREN'S BOOKS I LIVED IN FEAR OF DELIVERING THE WRONG ENVELOPE.

- BUT THIS IS NOT COLUMBUS ABOUT TO SAIL FROM SPAIN!!

EVENTUALLY, IN 1992, WHEN I WAS JUST READY TO DO SOMETHING ELSE, FED UP BY THE FACT THAT NOBODY SEEMED INTERESTED IN MY WORK, A VERY IMPORTANT MAGAZINE CALLED ME UP ASKING FOR A COMIC STRIP PAGE. IT WAS A SUCCESS. THE ENTIRE EDITING DEPARTMENT WAS IN TEARS...

ALTERED WOMEN

...SO I BECAME WHAT I'D ALWAYS WANTED TO BE...

A BLONDE

TIRED OF DESPERATELY LOOKING FOR LOVE, AND ABOUT TO BECOME A LESBIAN, I MET THE MAN OF MY LIFE

ONE HITCH: HE WAS DATING A FRIEND OF MINE

I LOST A FRIEND

LOVE MADE ME A HAPPY WOMAN. AT 37, TWENTY YEARS AFTER MY FIRST CHILD, I GAVE BIRTH TO MY THIRD, AND THOUGH MY SELF-ESTEEM GREW WITHOUT RESTRAINT AND TODAY MY HUMOR TRAVELS AROUND THE WORLD, THERE'S STILL SOMETHING I FAIL TO UNDERSTAND...

- HANDSOME!
- SENSITIVE!
- INTELLIGENT!
- FUNNY!
- WEALTHY!
- AND MY AGE!

HOW, IN THE END, EVERYTHING TURNED OUT SO WELL

maitena